Easy Christmas Mandalas
for Lefties !

to Color and Share with

People You Love

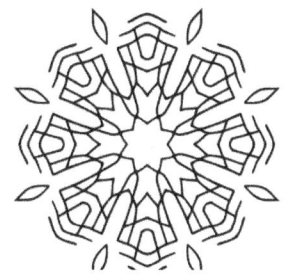

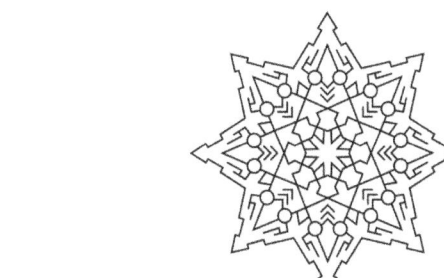

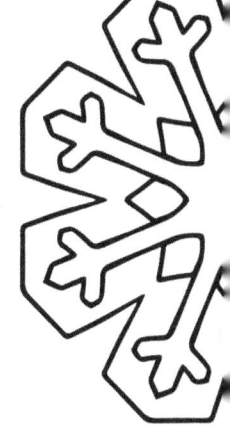

ISBN: 9798688944921

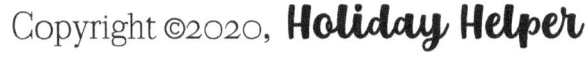

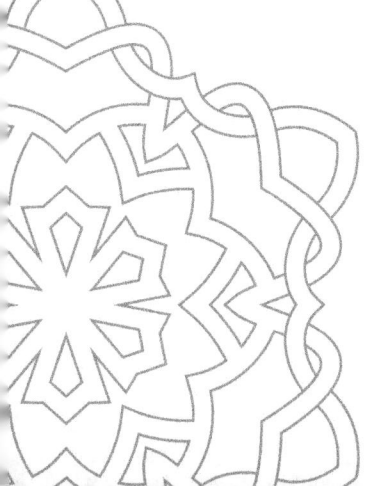

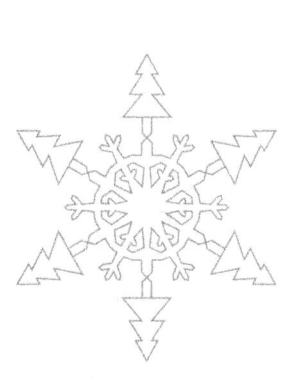

Oh, Christmas Tree!

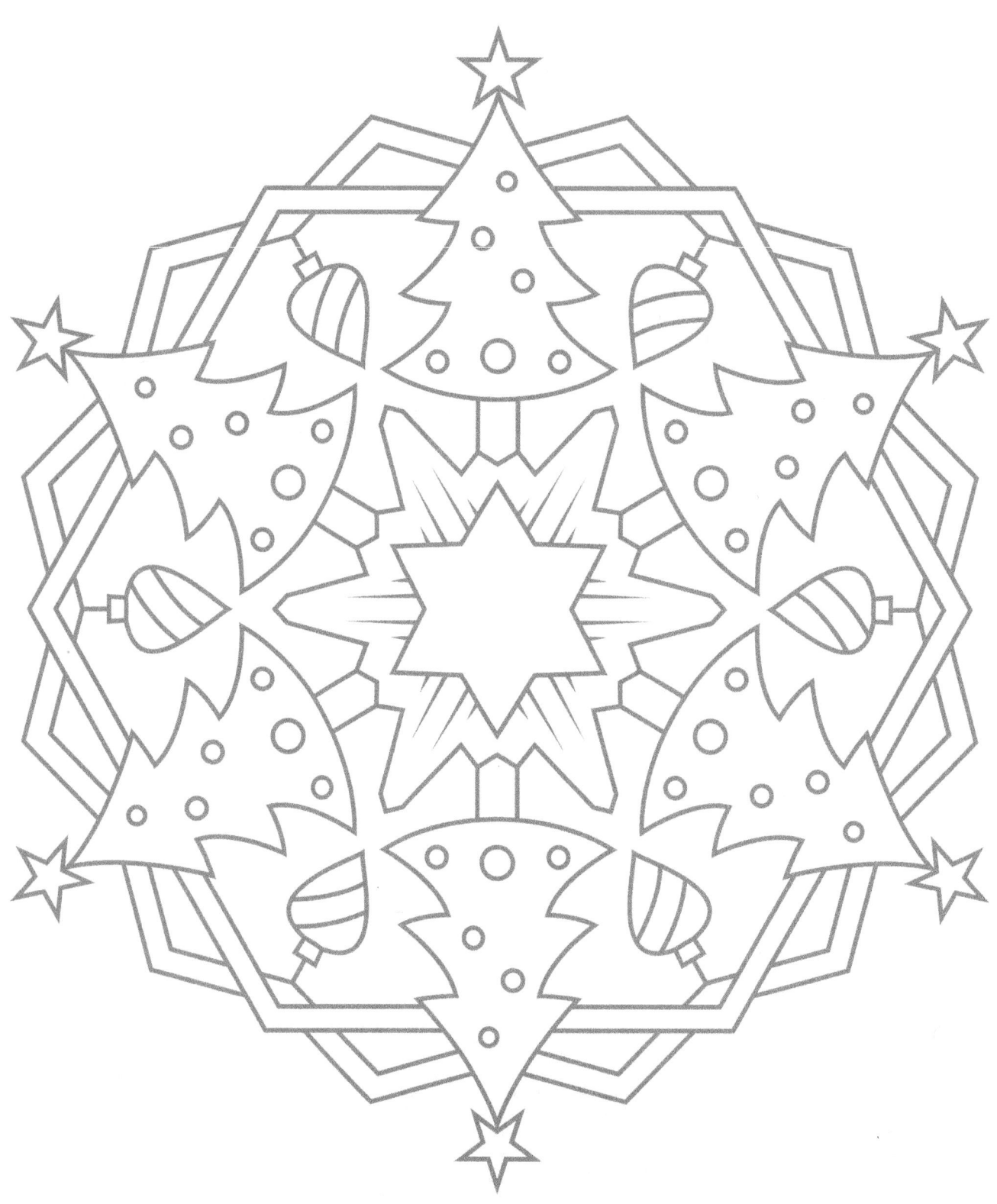

Bells

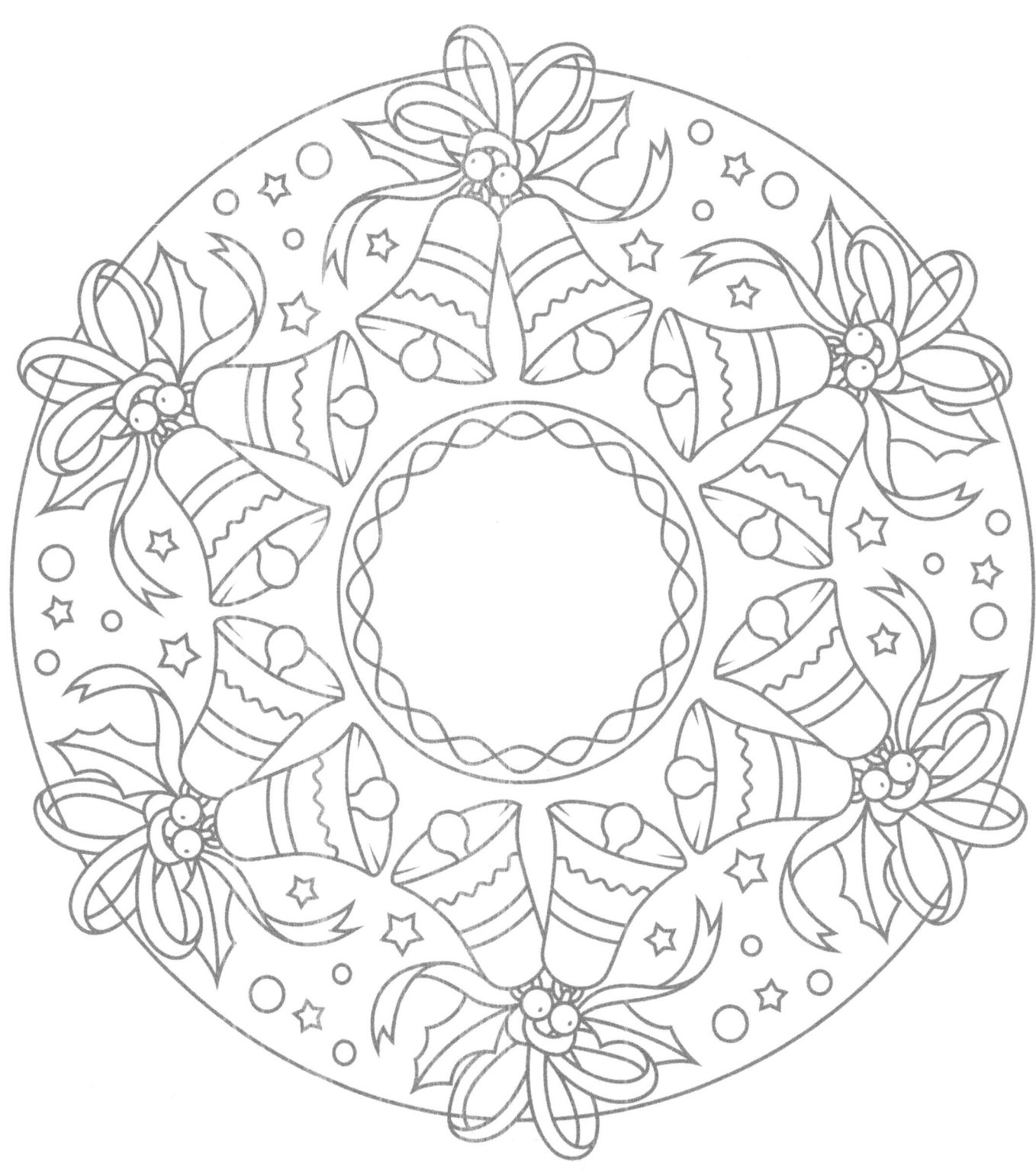

Penguins

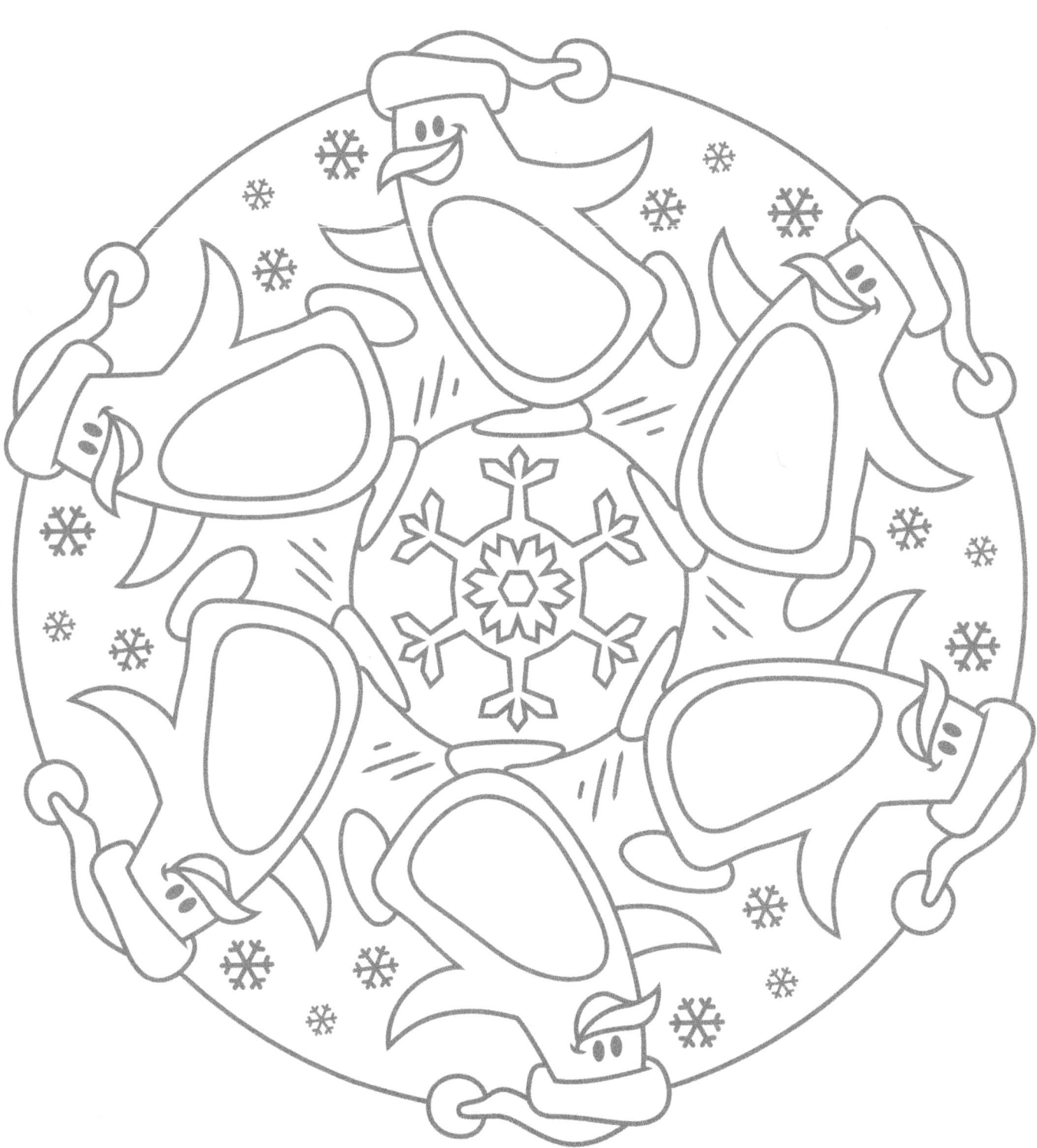

First Snowflake

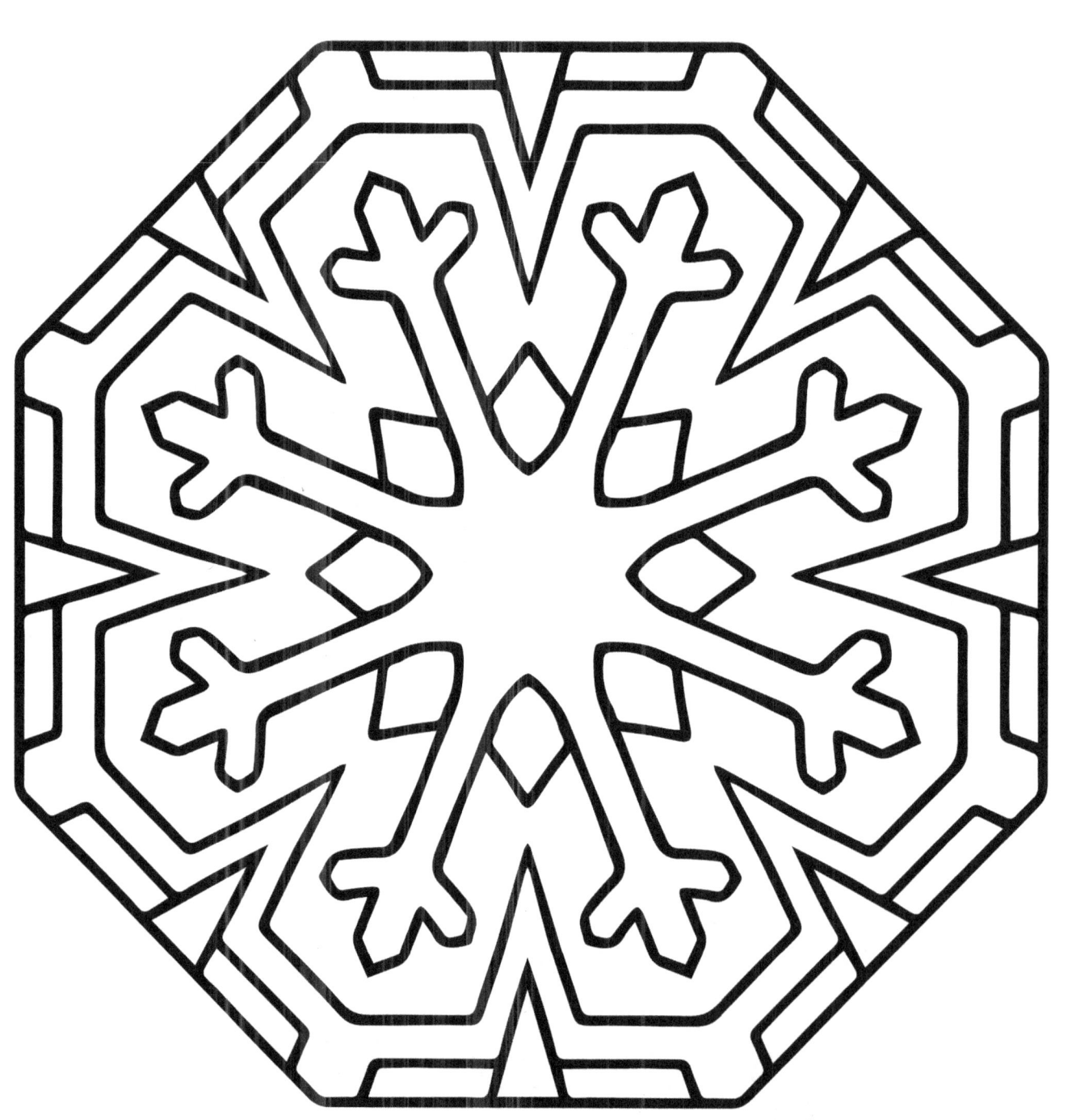

6 Leaf Flower

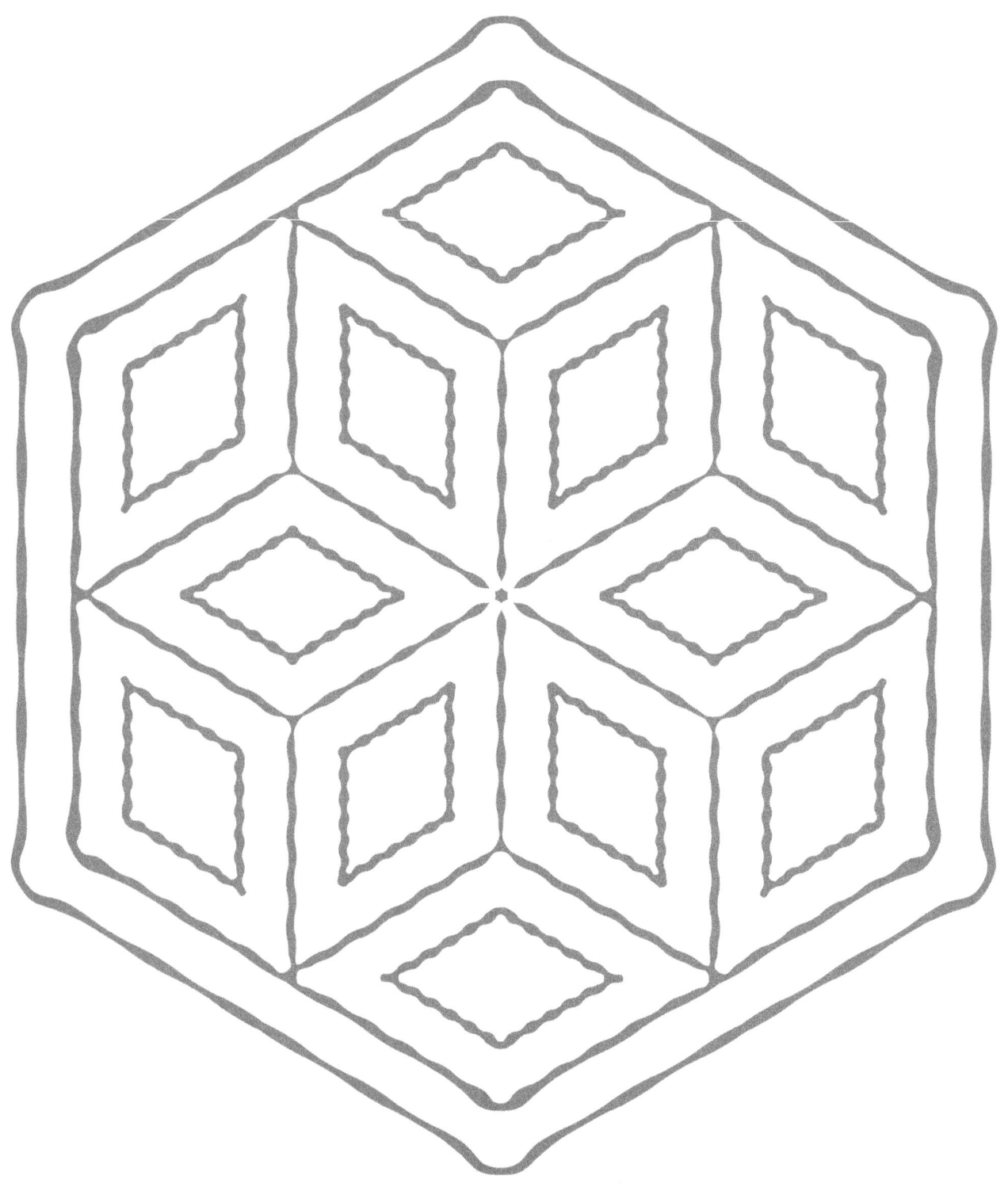

Snowmen

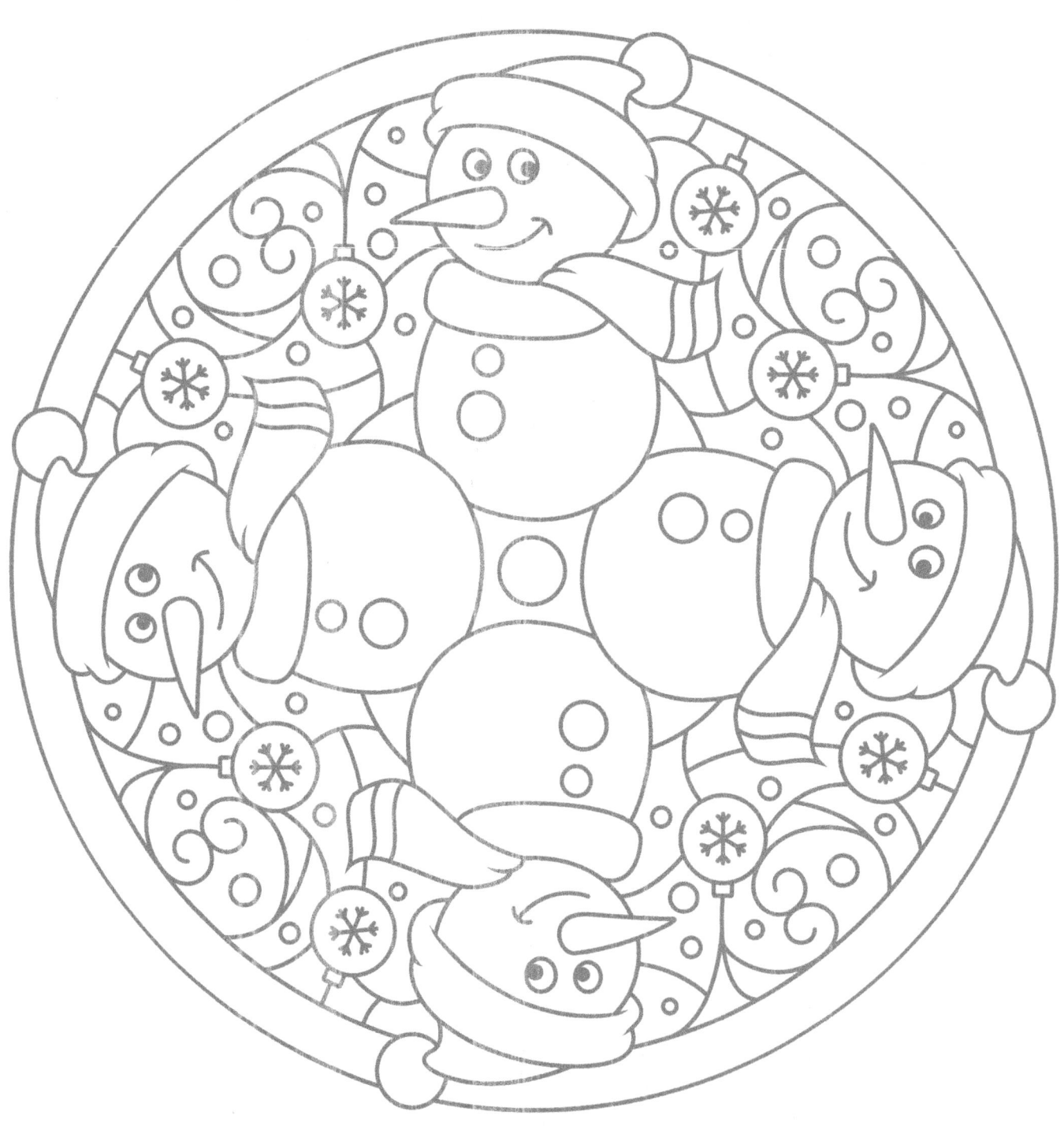

Holiday Wreath

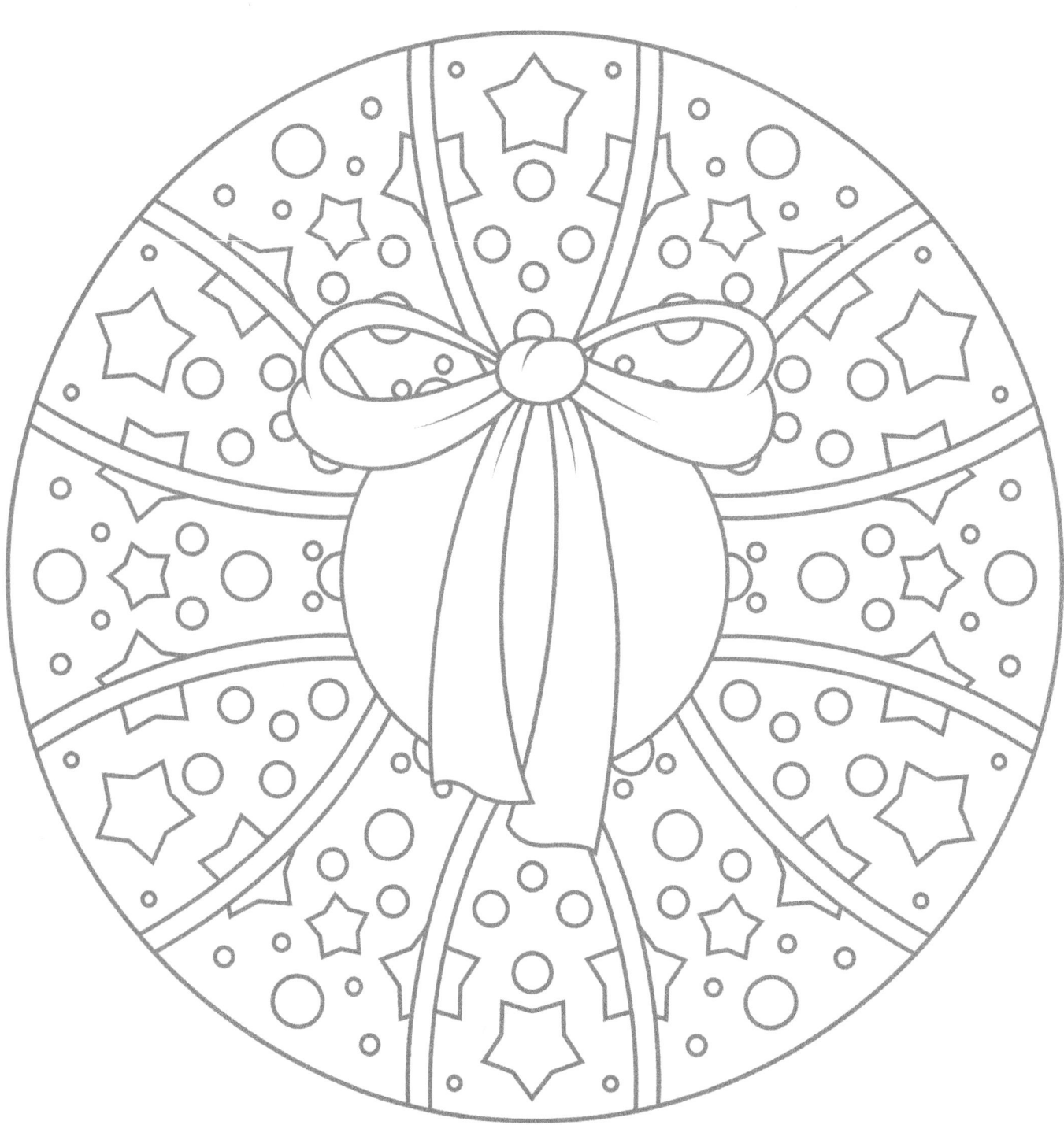

Candles

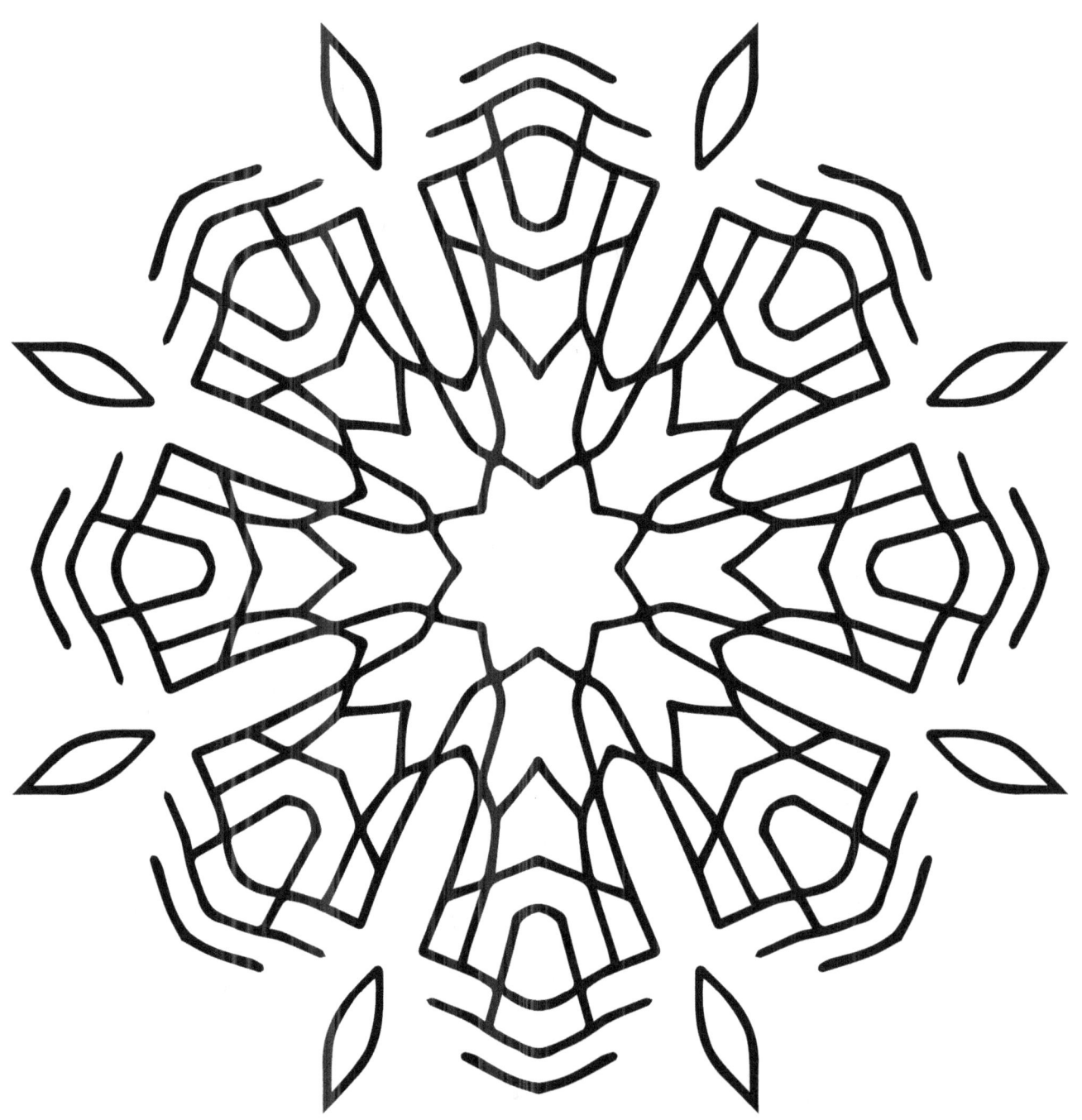

To All

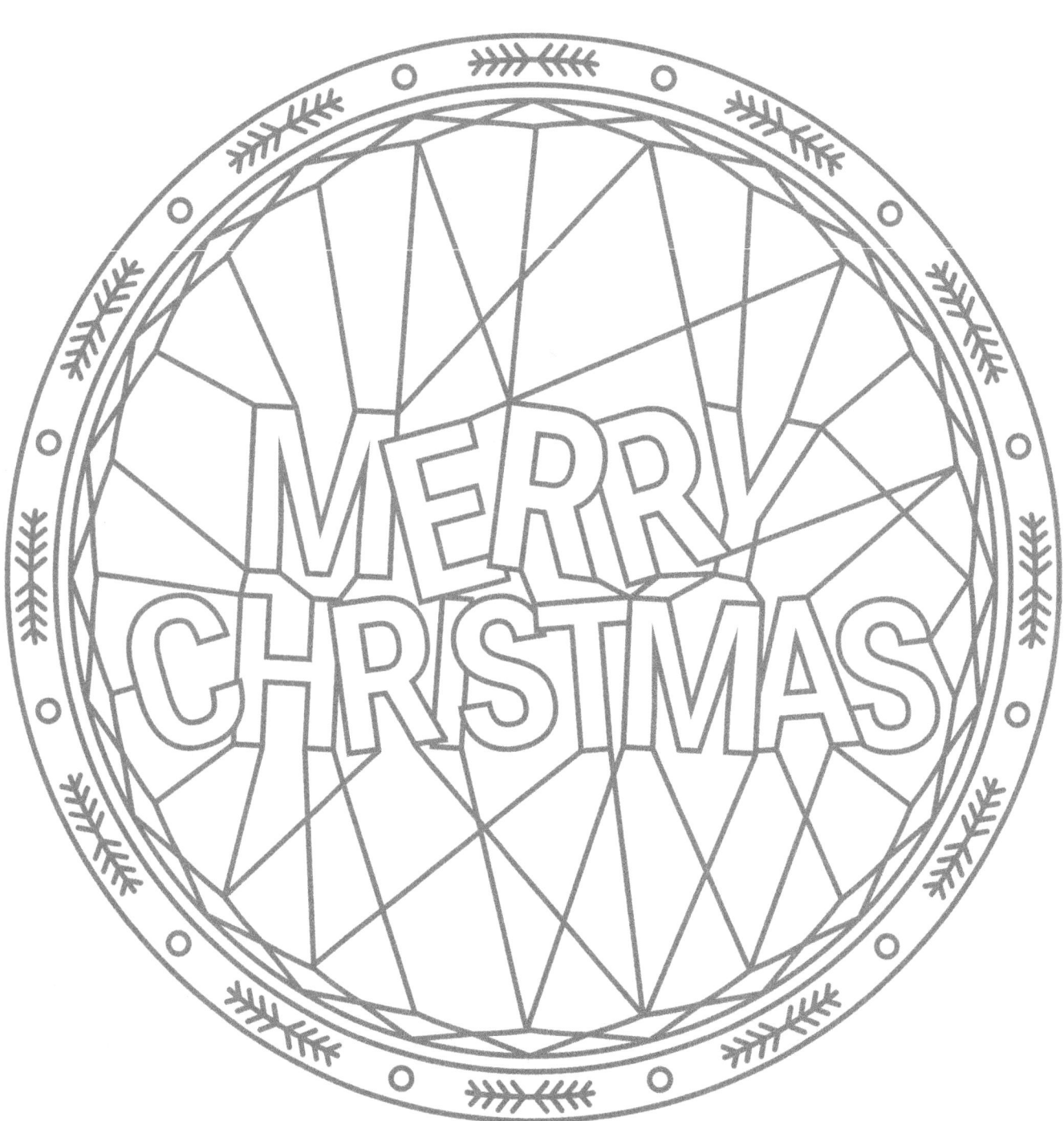

Santa

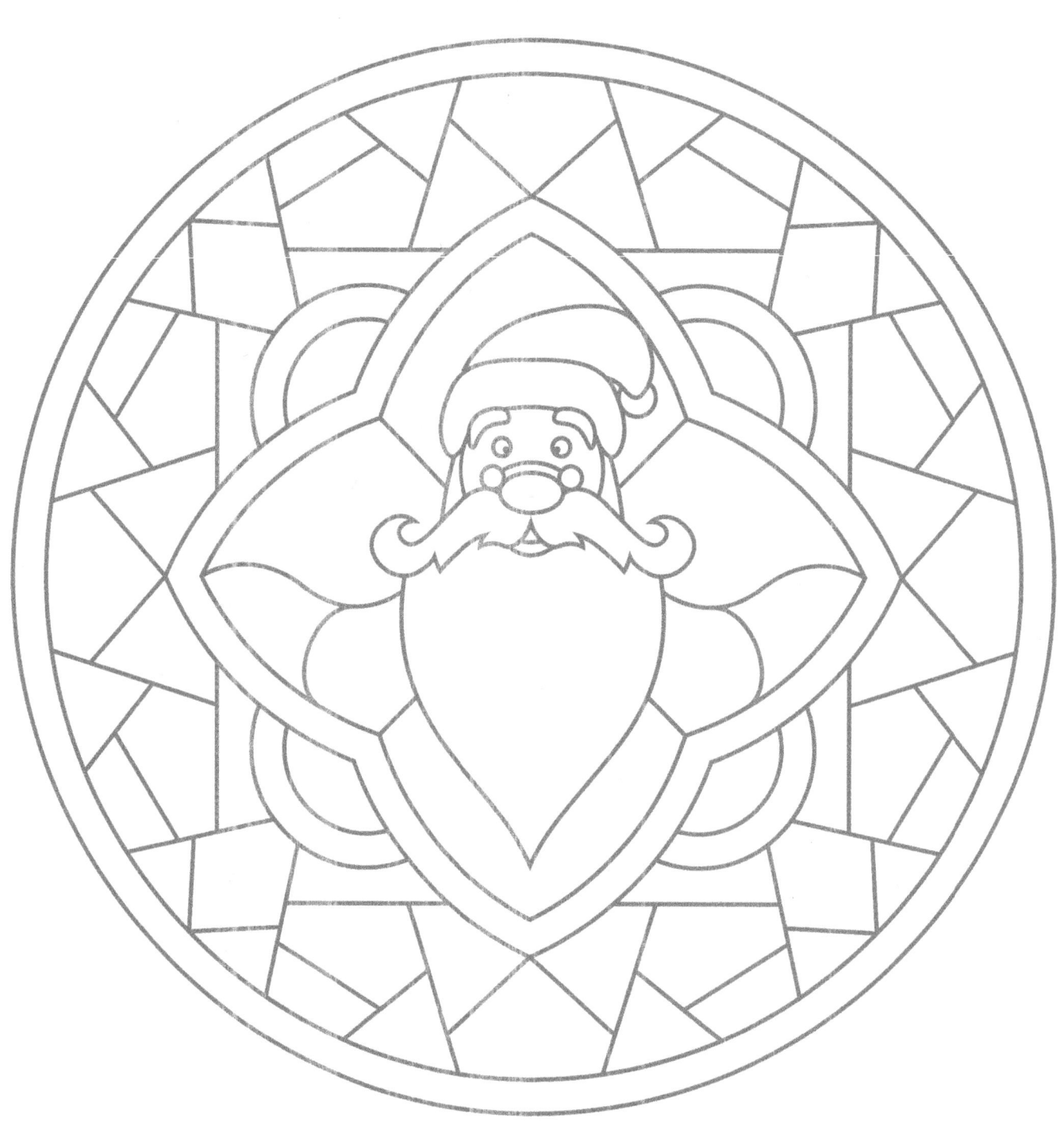

Little Angel

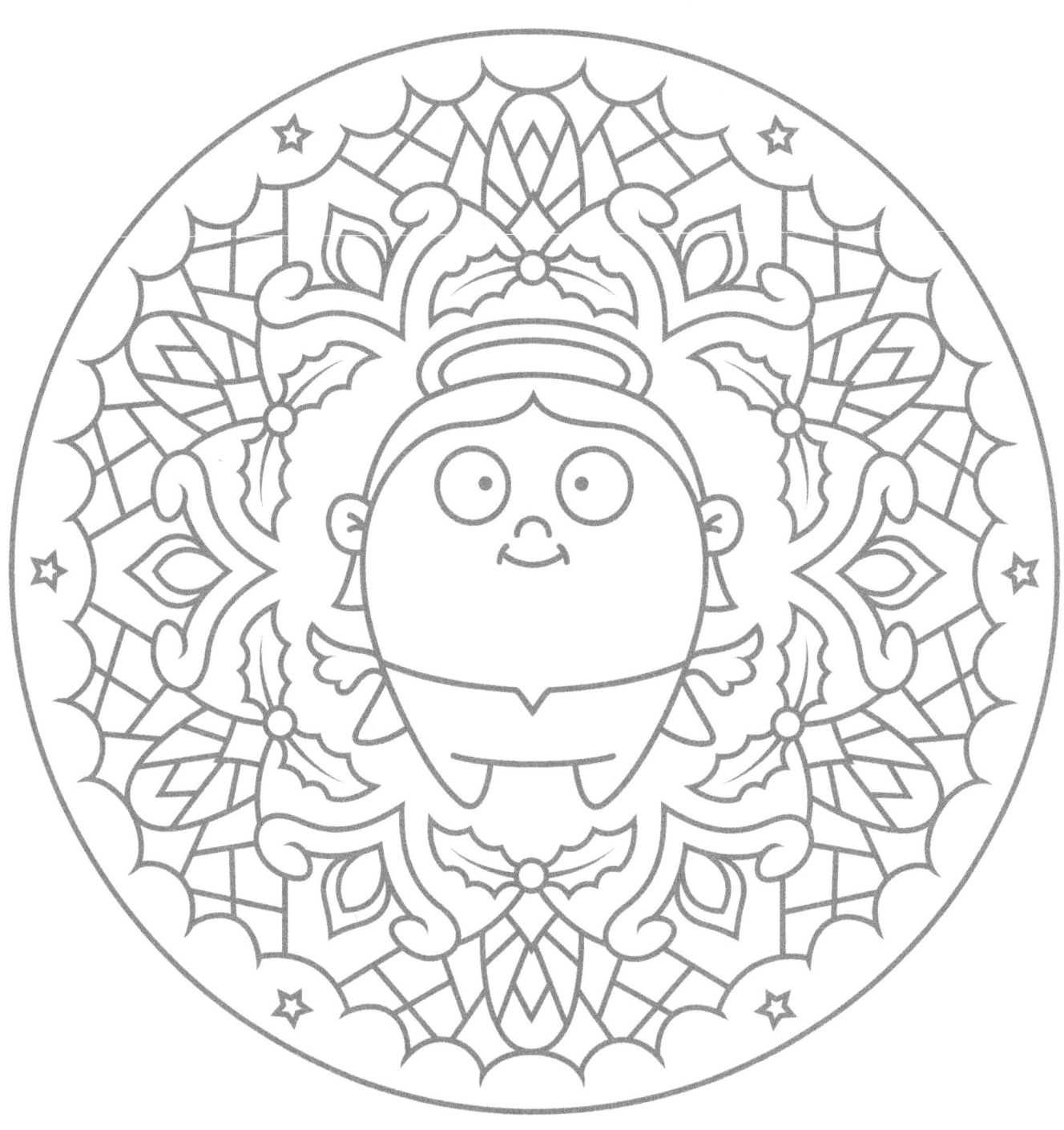

Circles and Branches

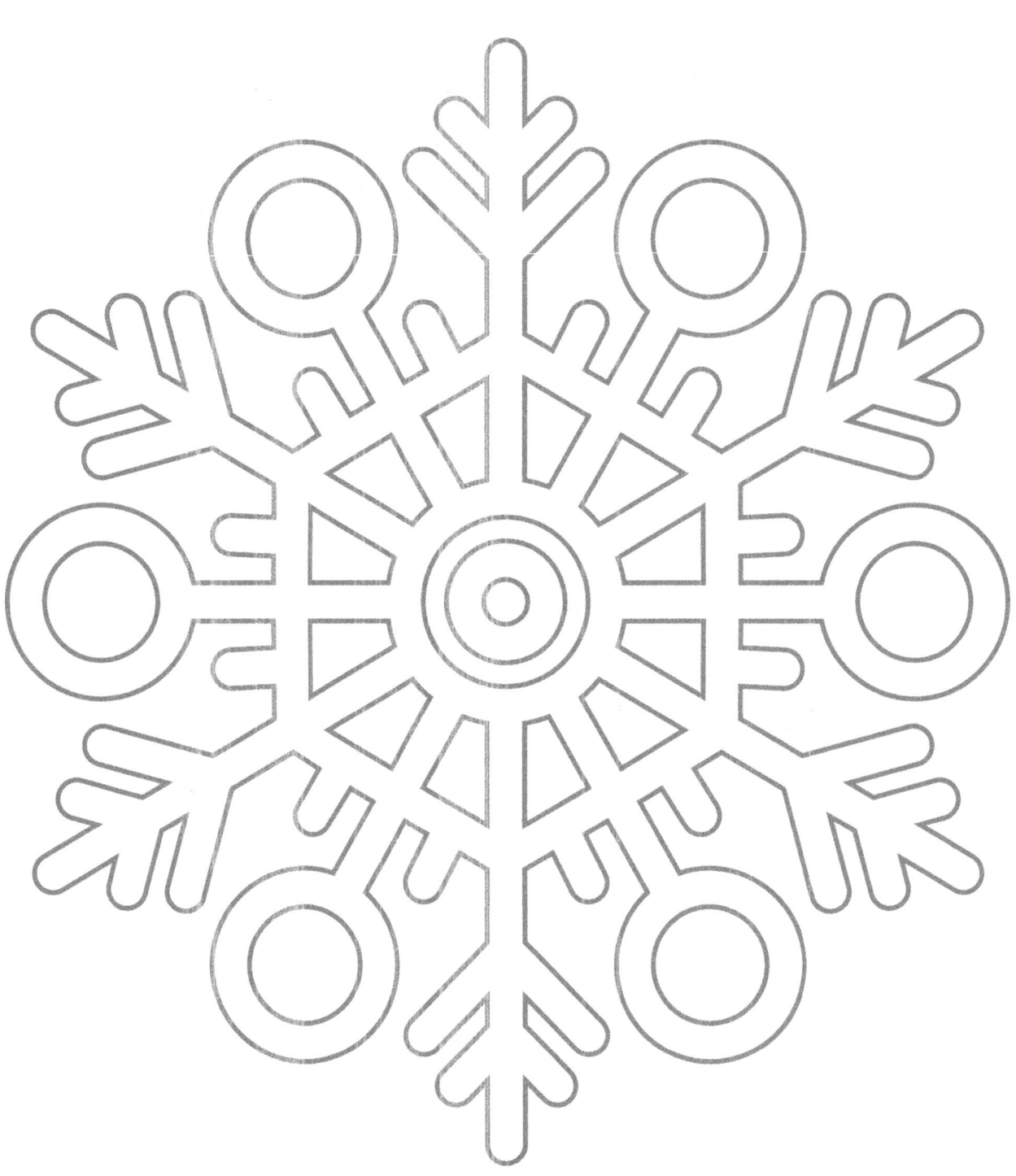

The Star

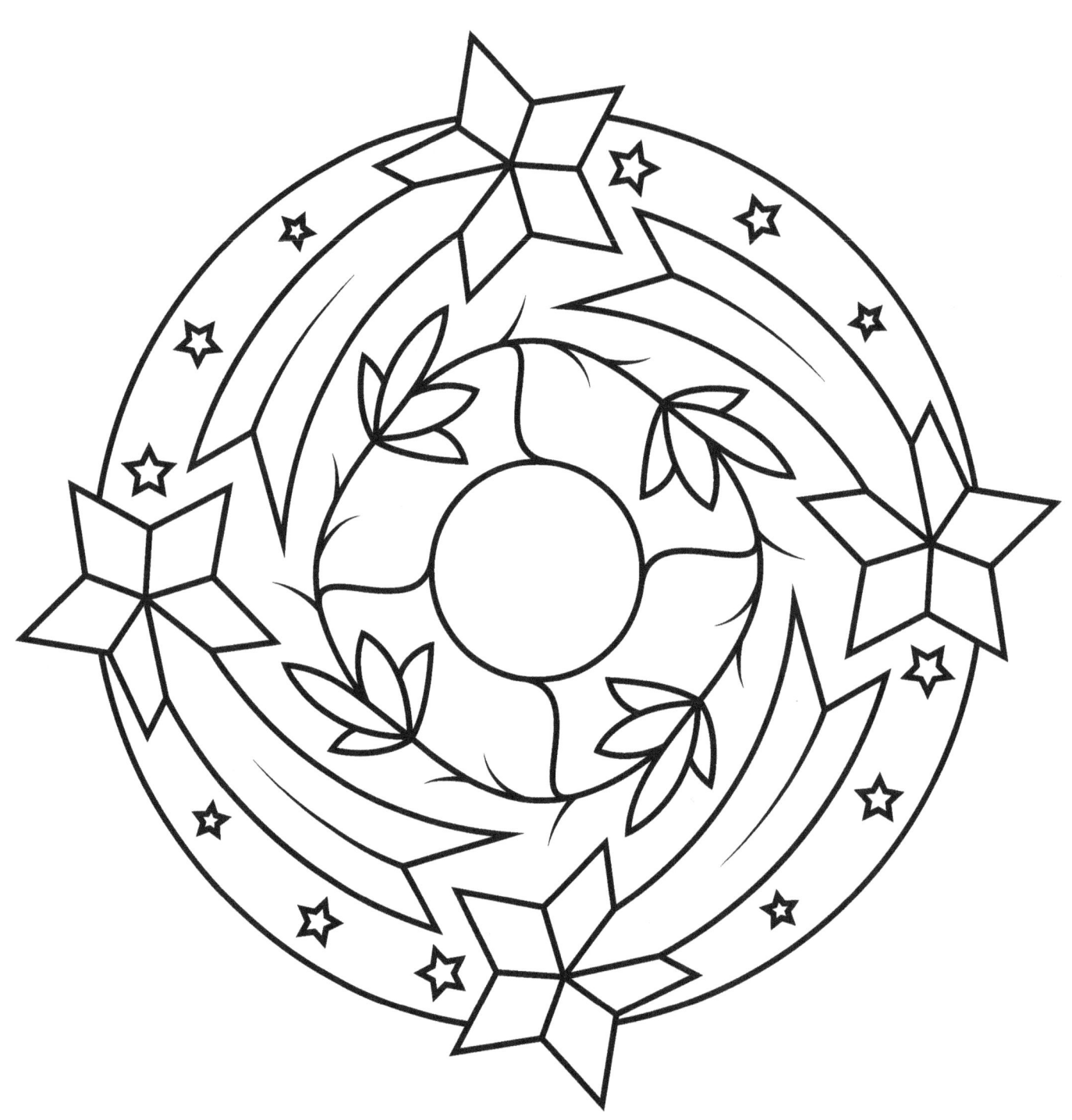

Gingerbread

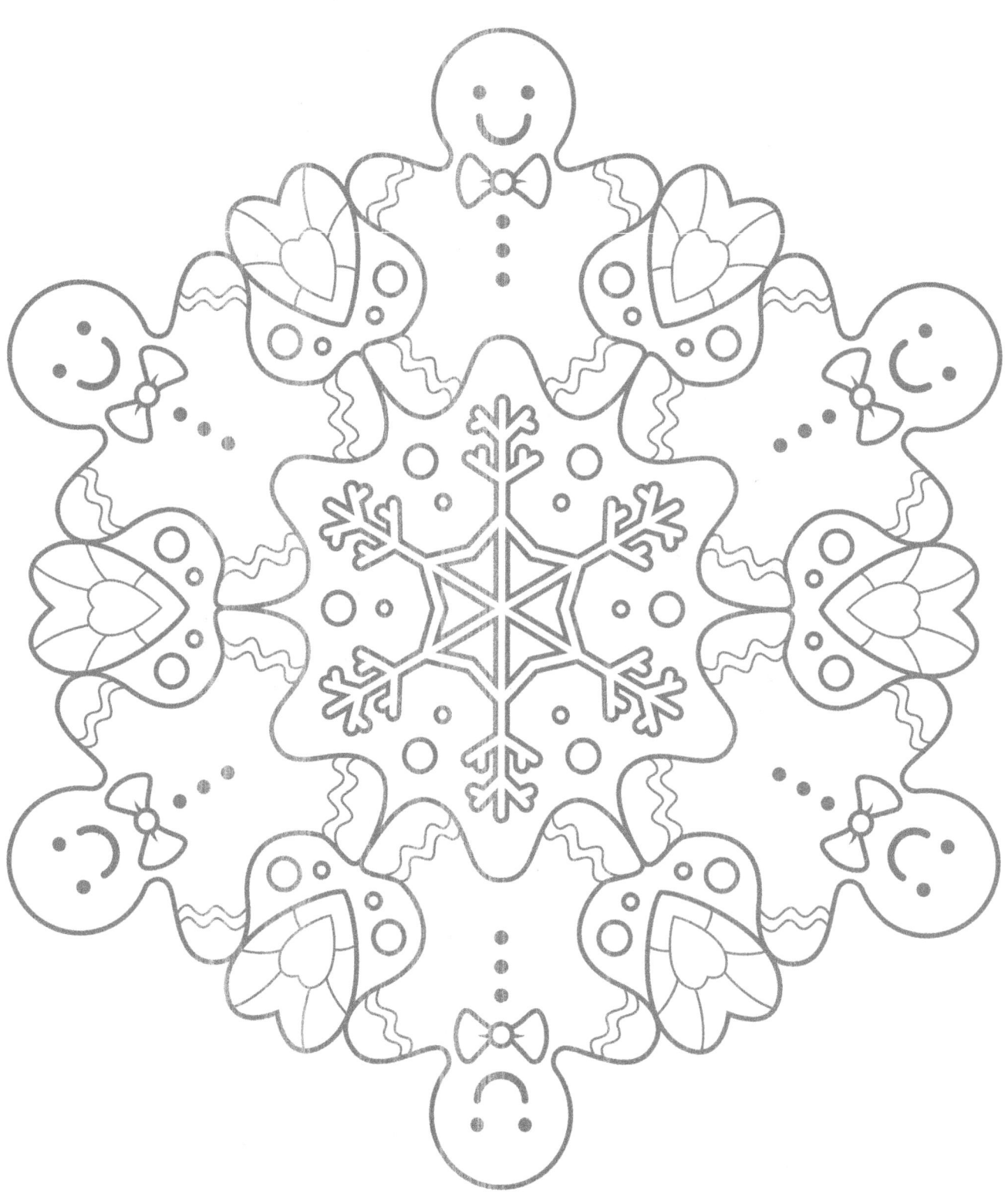

Christmas Flower

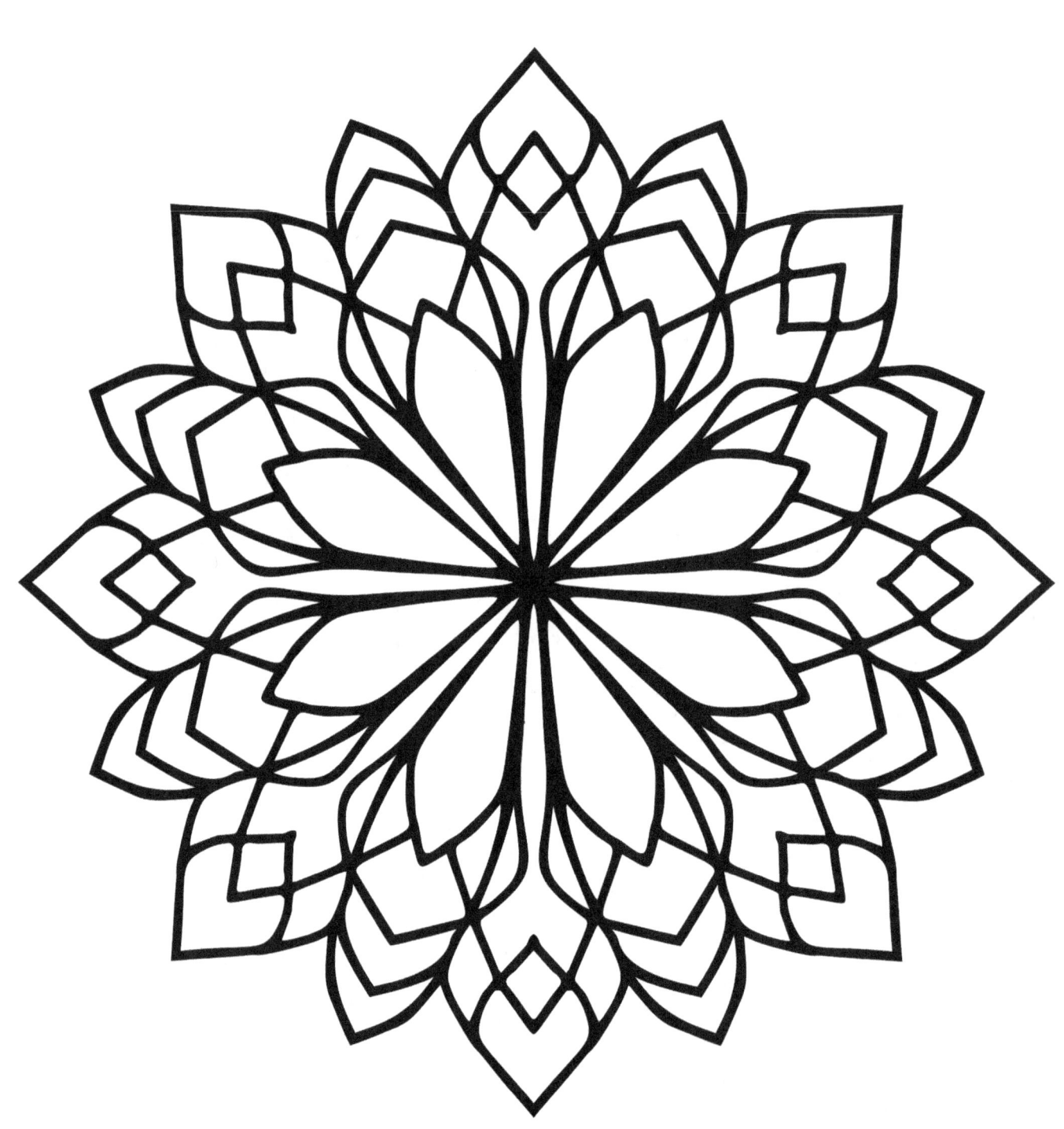

Tree Flake

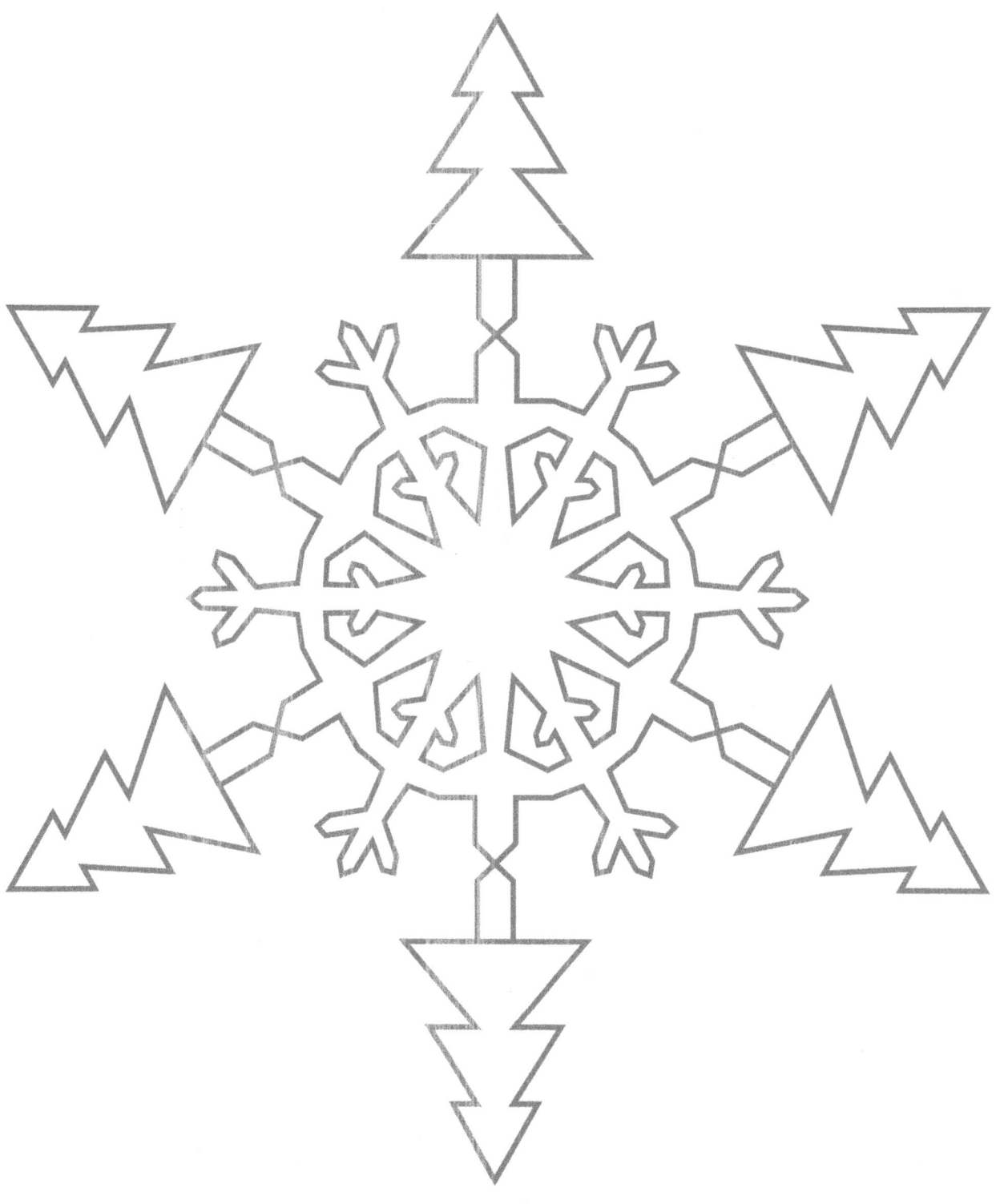

Reindeer Fun

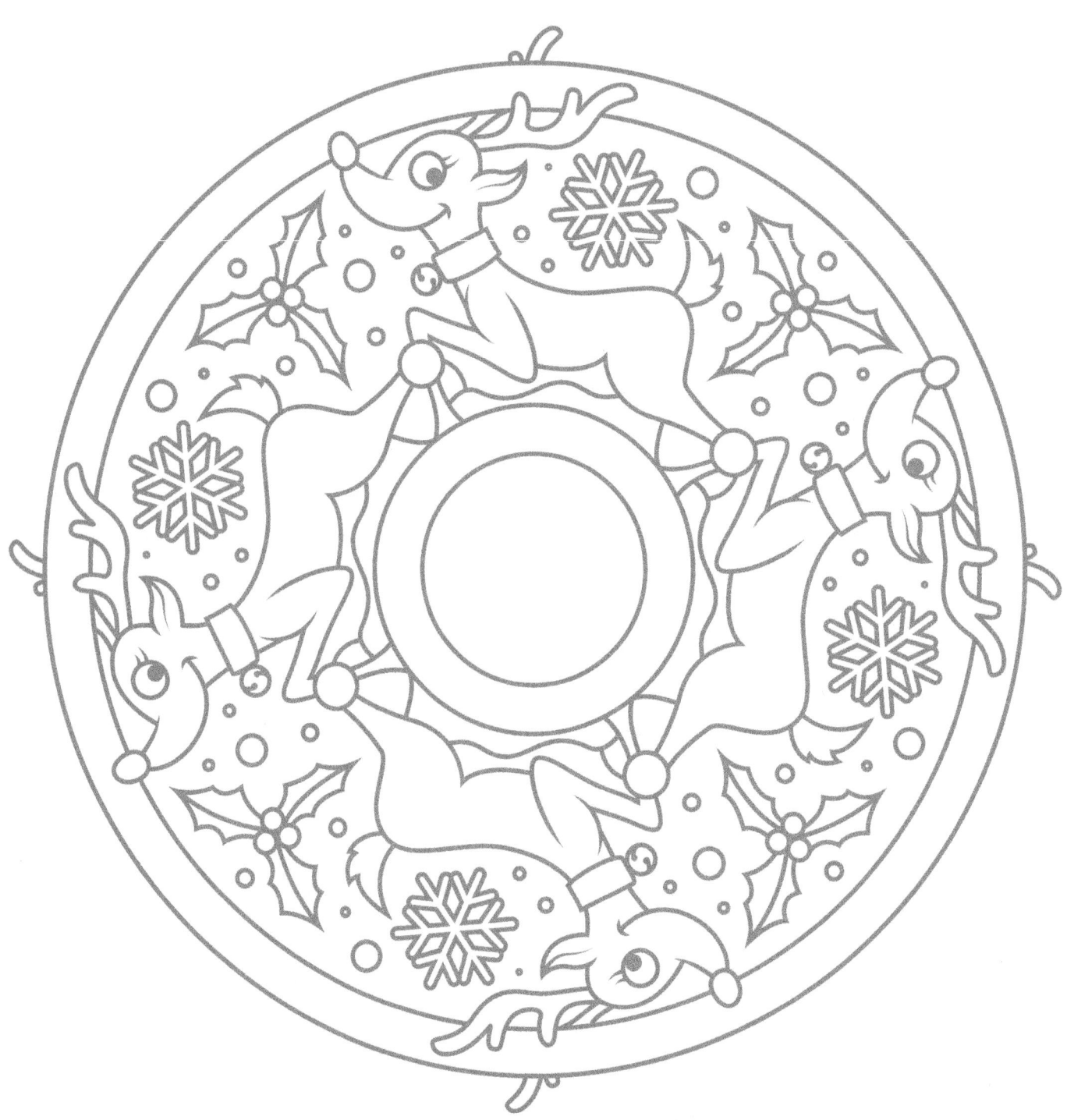

Leaves & Berries

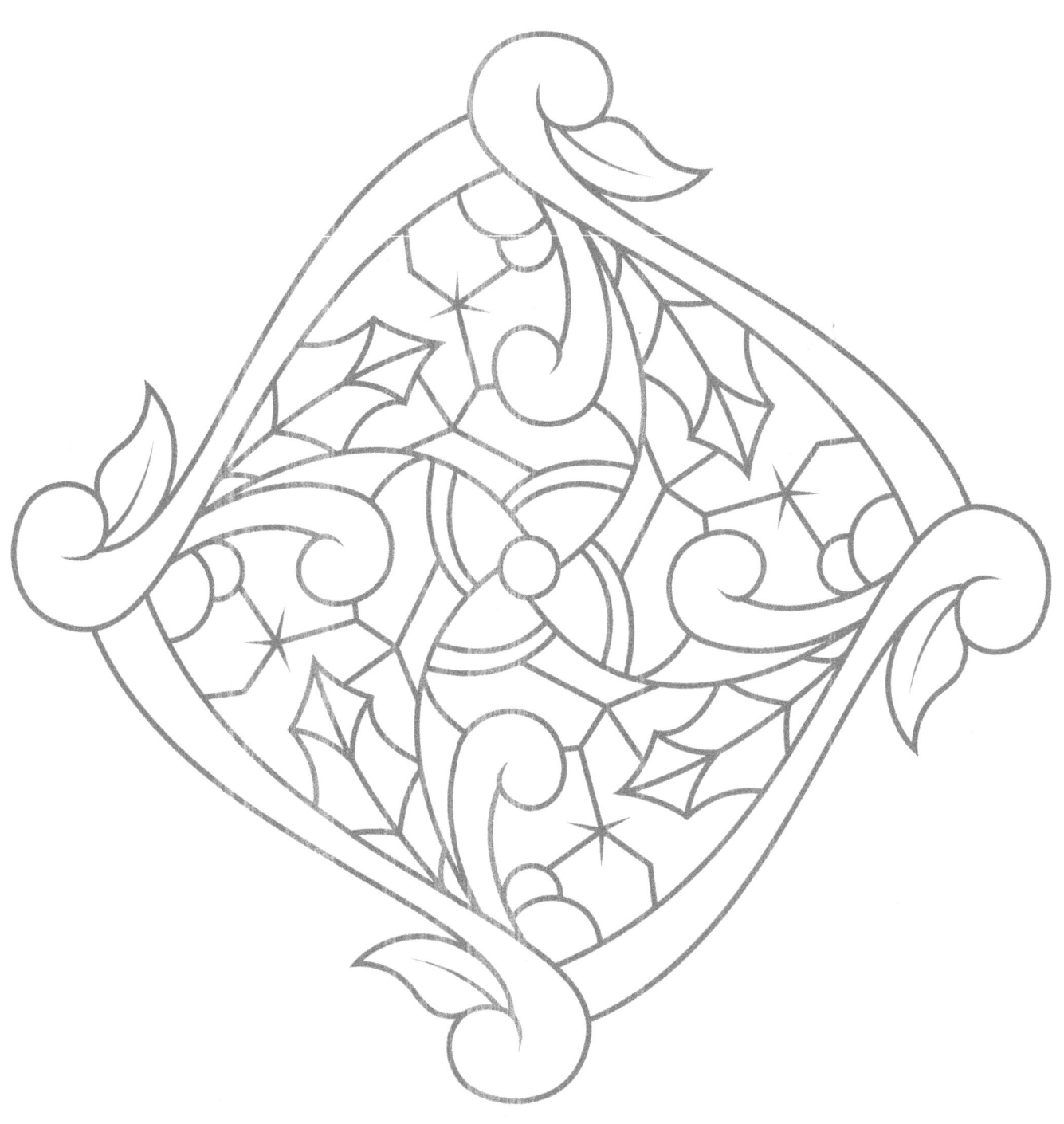

Chiming

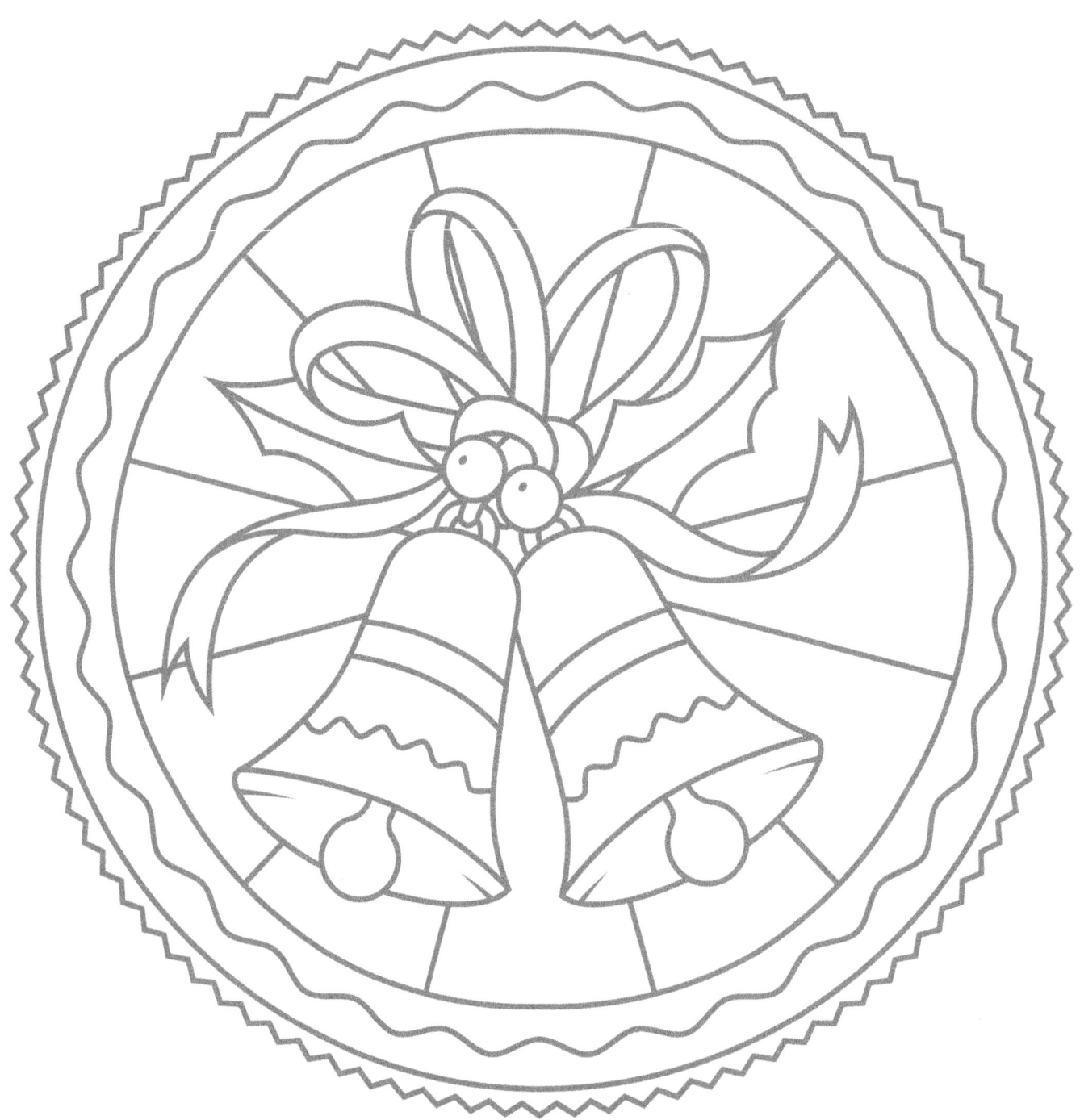

Ornaments

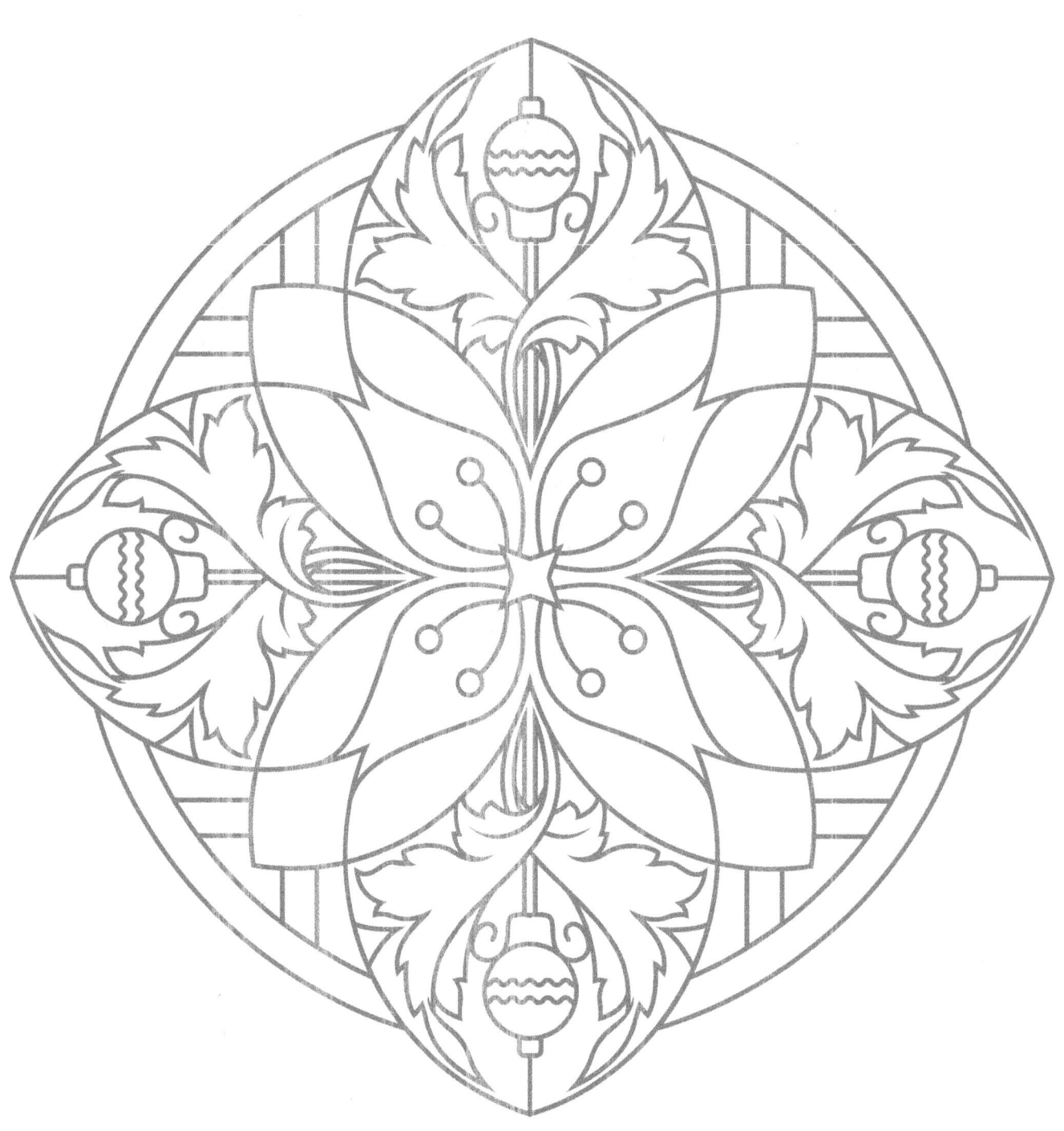

Abominable

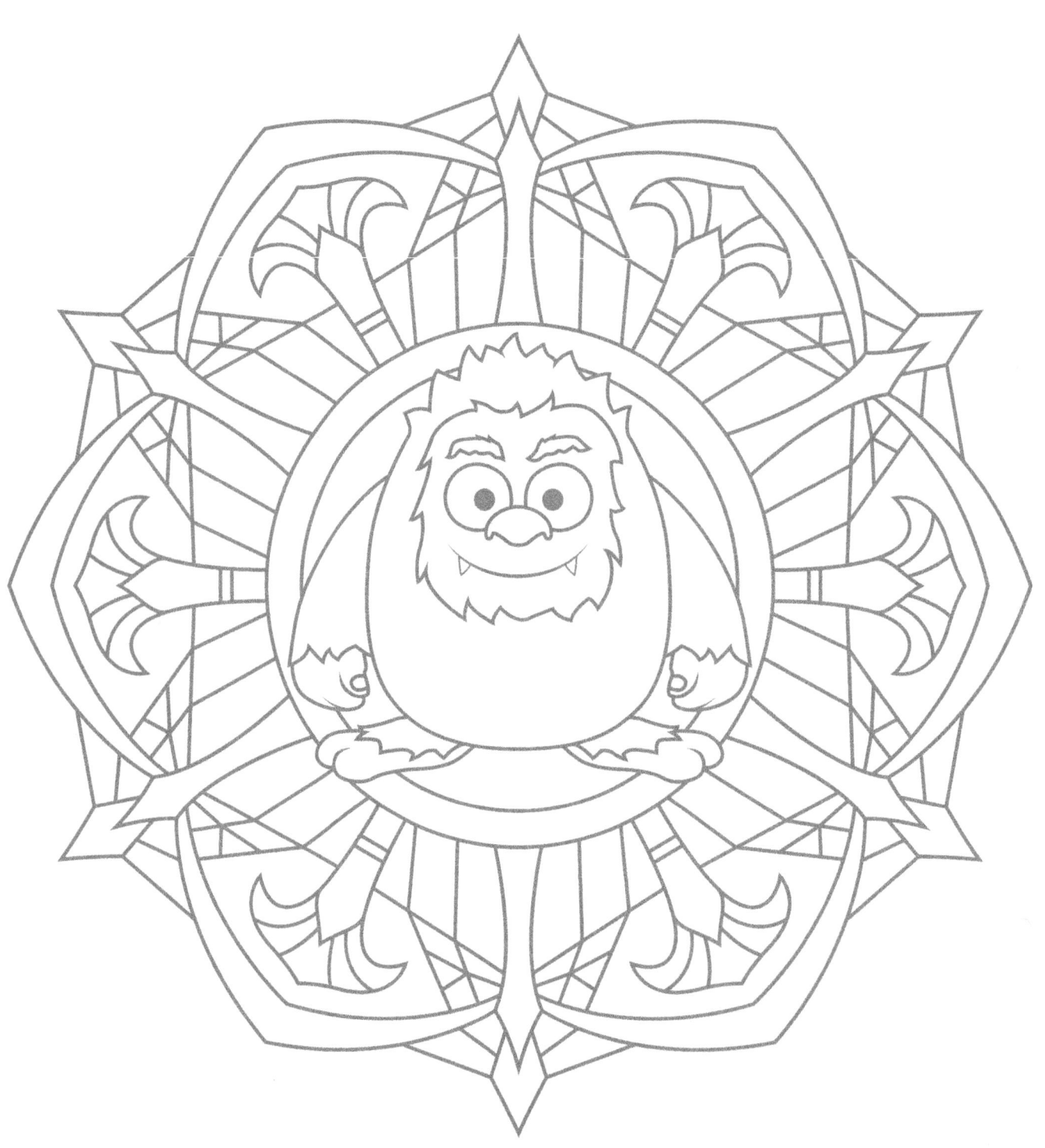

Snowflake Fort

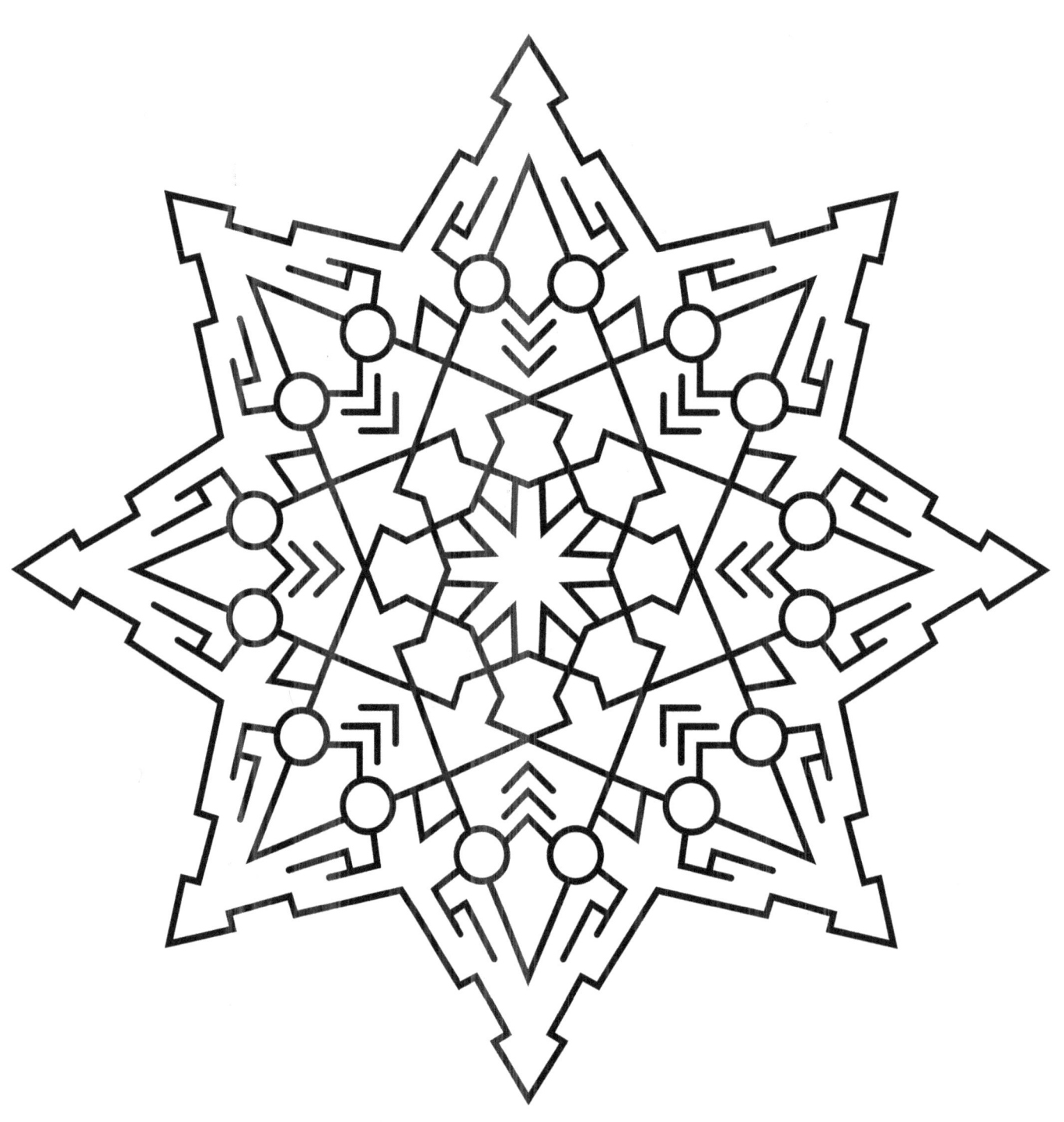

Candlelight

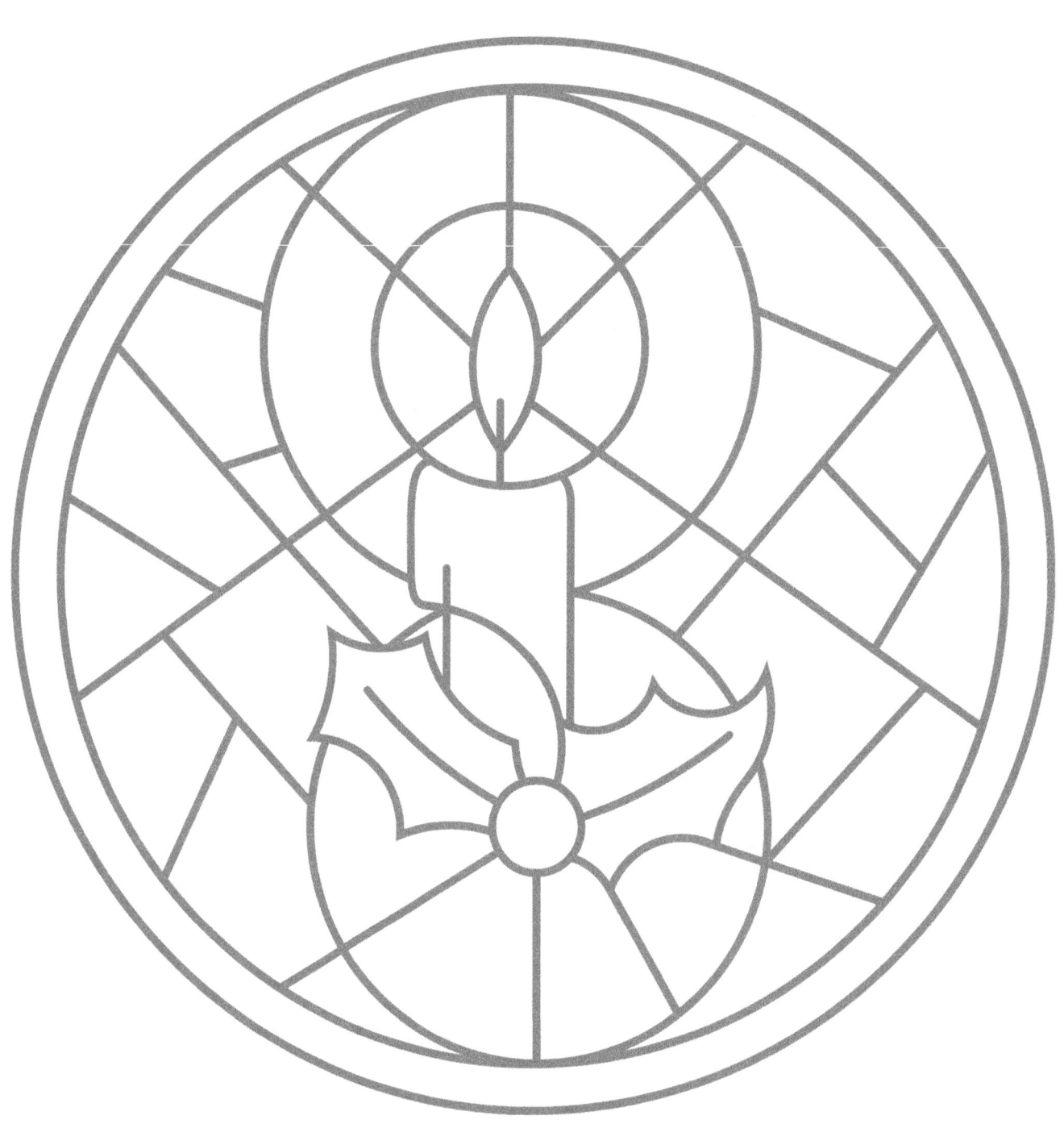

Good Night!

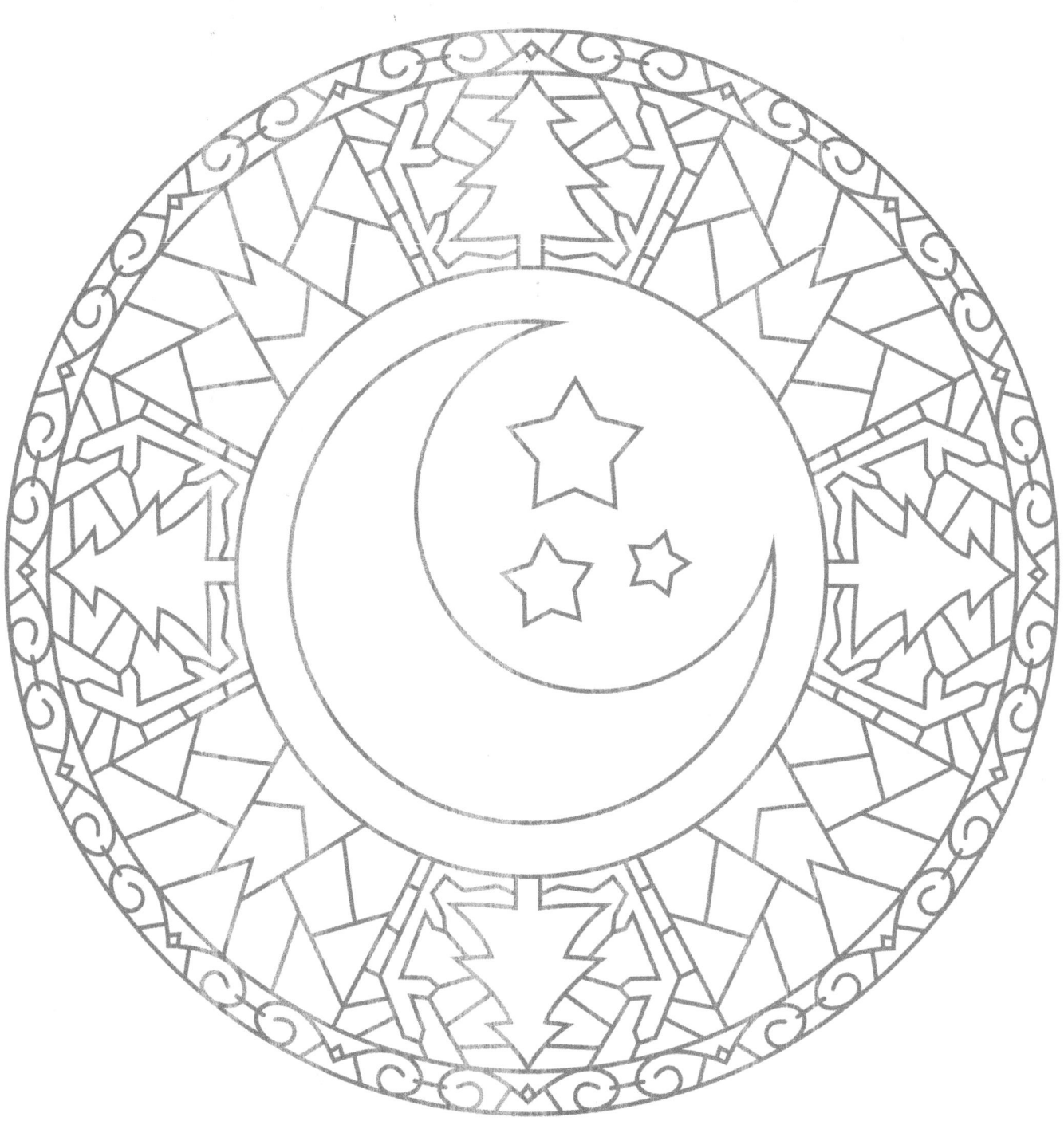

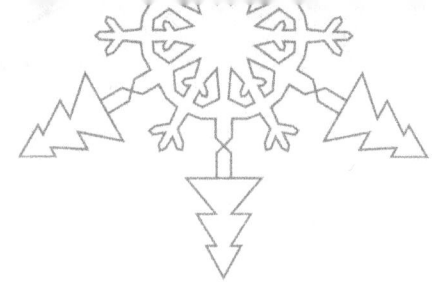
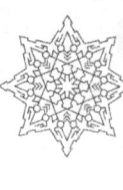

Like this Book?

Leave an Amazon Review

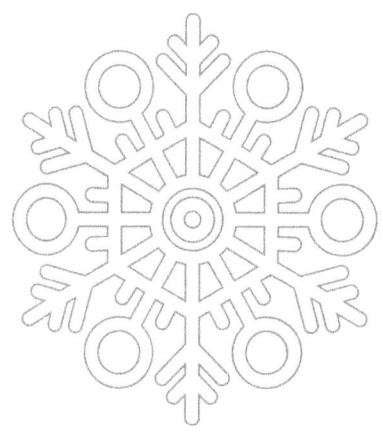

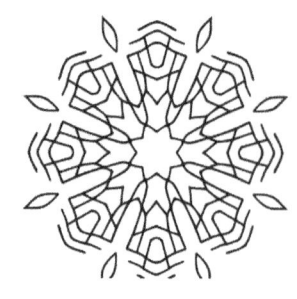

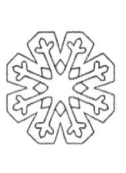

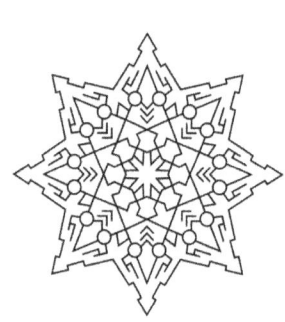

More books by Holiday Helper

Mini Easy Mandalas for Lefties 9798688948707
Easy Mandalas for Kids 9798688942934